The _most_ _excellent_ book of how to do
card tricks

Peter Eldin
Illustrated by Rob Shone

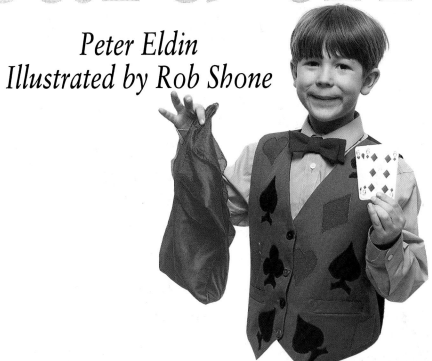

Copper Beech Books
Brookfield, Connecticut

© Aladdin Books Ltd 1996
Designed and produced by
Aladdin Books Ltd
28 Percy Street
London WIP 0LD

*First published in the United
States in 1996 by*
Copper Beech Books,
an imprint of
The Millbrook Press
2 Old New Milford Road
Brookfield, Connecticut 06804

Editor Katie Roden
Design David West Children's
Book Design
Designer Edward Simkins
Illustrator Rob Shone
Photography Roger Vlitos

Printed in Belgium

Library of Congress Cataloging-in-
Publication Data
Eldin, Peter. The most excellent
book of how to do card tricks / by
Peter Eldin : illustrated by Rob
Shone.
p. cm.
Includes Index.
Summary:
Presents instructions for
performing an array of card tricks,
with practical advice on shuffling,
manner of display, and other card-
handling tips.
ISBN 0-7613-0525-4 (lib. bdg.)
ISBN 0-7613-0504-1 (pbk.)
1. Card tricks--Juvenile literature.
[1. Card tricks. 2. Magic tricks.]
I. Shone, Rob, ill. II. Title.
GV1549.E483 1996   96-7973
795.4'38-- 5 4 3 2   CIP AC

CONTENTS

INTRODUCTION

Card tricks are a lot of fun.
You can entertain your friends... and yourself!
And you don't need lots of equipment – just a deck
of cards. Some of the tricks in this book use special
cards, but they are all easy to make.

The most important part of a card trick is
the way in which you present it, so you
should practice it until you can do it without
thinking. The more you practice, the better you
will be; the better you are, the more you will enjoy doing it; and the
more you enjoy doing it, the more your friends will enjoy watching you!

As you read the book, look for these symbols:
★ shows the secret preparation you need to make
before you perform your tricks.
✔ will give you tips on how to perfect
your card craft.

Have fun with this book – and have
fun with your card tricks!

Tricks of the TRADE

Taking Care of Your Cards

Playing cards are inexpensive to buy, but the most inexpensive ones may not last long. To make your own, use bright paints and stiff cardboard. Always use strong, clean cards, and don't play cards with the decks you use for your tricks – they will get dirty and sticky.

Keep Them Clean!

The best way to clean your cards is to use a piece of bread. Roll it into a ball and rub it gently over any marks. For stubborn marks, use a small amount of powdered soap on a damp cloth. Don't use too much water and don't try this on cheap cards.

Your Card Table

A table or another flat surface is also important for some of your tricks, especially if you need to prepare cards or decks before your performance.

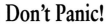

Don't Panic!

Don't try to learn too many tricks at once. Just choose two or three and practice them really well. When you can do them properly, start learning some of the other tricks. If you make a mistake when performing a trick, the best thing to do is to ignore it and carry on.

Magic Fingers

If you find a trick hard, try changing the position of your fingers. Everyone's hands are different and what may be easy for someone else can be difficult for you.

That's Entertainment!

Don't just stand in front of your audience and do your tricks. Try entertaining them by telling stories or jokes. Smile while you perform your tricks. If you look uncomfortable, your audience will feel the same. Be confident – the audience will believe you really do have magic powers!

Fancy WORK

Show the audience that you have magic hands!

Swivel Cut (A cut is a way of dividing the deck)

1 Hold the deck in your left hand, with your thumb at one end and the first two fingers at the other. The third finger is at the front left corner and the little finger is at the side of the deck to help keep all the cards straight.

2 Bring your right forefinger to the corner closest to you. Push half of the cards forward. The left third finger acts as a hinge.

3 As your right hand moves forward, turn it palm upward. The cards you have pushed off will swivel and drop into your right hand.

4 Put the remaining cards in your left hand on top of those in your right and the cut is complete.

Forefinger Cut

1 Hold the deck in your right hand, between the thumb at one end and the second and third fingers at the other.

2 With your forefinger at the front left corner, lift half of the cards.

3 Push the cards against your thumb for stability, then move the top half of the deck to the left.

4 When the top half has moved about a half inch to the left, grasp the corner between your left thumb and forefinger.

5 Move your left hand to the left as you pull the cards from the top. Let the top half fall into the palm of your left hand, then place the rest of the deck on top.

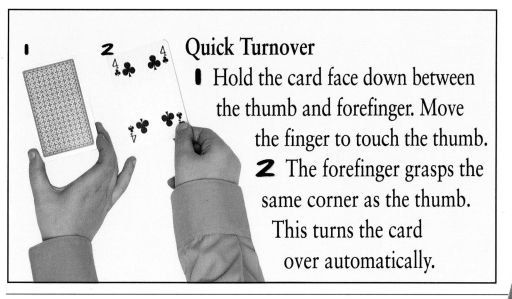

Quick Turnover

1 Hold the card face down between the thumb and forefinger. Move the finger to touch the thumb.

2 The forefinger grasps the same corner as the thumb. This turns the card over automatically.

May the Force BE WITH YOU

Make a spectator take the card you want ("forcing").

Any Number

★ *Before your show, put the card you wish to force on top of the deck.*

❶ Pick up the deck and ask a member of the audience for a number between 10 and 30.

2 Count that number of cards from the deck. Put them in a pile.

3 Place this pile at an angle on top of the rest of the cards.

4 Lift the top portion of the deck and show the spectator the card on the bottom of that portion. Ask him or her to remember it.

✔ *You have "forced" the card you want, but the spectator appears to have a free choice. You can now perform a trick such as Manuscript Magic (see page 26), knowing which card will be used.*

Mathematical Force

★ *Place the card you want to force in the ninth position from the top of the deck.*

"Force" card is ninth in deck

1 Ask a member of the audience for a number between 10 and 20.

2 Count off the chosen number of cards, one at a time, onto the table.

3 Add together the digits of the chosen number (if, for example, the number is 14, you should add 1 and 4 to make 5). Count that number of cards from the pile of cards you have just dealt.

4 Ask the spectator to take the next card. It seems that the spectator has had a completely free choice. In fact the final card is your "force" card. The "force" works mathematically.

✔ As you perform, keep reminding the spectator that his or her choice of number is a free one.

2

4

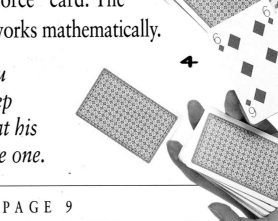

Quick CHANGE

A playing card changes its value – by magic!

★ *You will need: 3 playing cards; glue.*

1. Fold two of the cards exactly in half. Glue the two folded cards back to back for half of their length.

2. Stick the two glued cards onto the face of the third card to make a card with a movable flap. When the flap is held flat to the top, it will show the face of one card; if it is pushed down, another card will be seen.

1 Hold the special card in your left hand, with the flap facing away from you.

2 Move your right hand over the card, moving downward. As you do so, push the flap from the top position to the bottom. This secret move is hidden by your right hand.

It looks as if you just wave your hand over the card and it changes magically!

Turn AROUND

Reveal your amazing brain power!

★ *You will need: 4 or more face cards (Jacks, Queens, or Kings).*

1. *On most face cards, the white margin on one edge is wider than that on the other. Take out all the face cards with different margins.*

2. *Put the face cards face up on the table, making sure that all the wider margins are on the left.*

❙ Ask a volunteer to turn one card around, end for end, while you leave the room.

2 When you come back, look for the card with the wider margin on the right – that is the one that has been moved.

✔ *If you pick up the card, put it back with the wide margin on the left, then do the trick again. Repeat it once – the audience may figure it out!*

Spots before your EYES

Have you got one card – or four?

★ *You will need: a piece of cardboard (6 in x 8 in); a pencil or paint.*
On one side of the card, draw two diamonds. On the other side, draw five diamonds. Draw the diamonds in the positions shown in the pictures

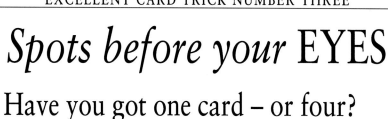

❙ Hold the card in your left hand with the two diamonds facing the audience. Make sure your fingers cover the blank space at the bottom. Say "Three of Diamonds" when you show the card to the audience. Although only two diamonds can be seen, they will think there are three if you say the words with confidence.

2 Bring your right hand up and use it to turn the card over. Practice this so that your fingers cover the blank space on the five-diamond side. Show this side of the card to the audience. The audience will think that there is another diamond under your fingers. Say "Six."

3 With your left hand, turn the card over again. Make sure that your fingers cover the lower of the two diamonds. It now looks like a single diamond. As you show this side of the card again, say "One."

4 With your right hand, turn the card over again. This time your fingers must be positioned so that they cover the diamond in the center. Say "Four."

3

4

✔ *Practice this trick so you know exactly where to put your hands. Try to perform it smoothly, quickly, and confidently.*

The Mischievous JOKER

The Joker changes into another card!

★ *You will need: a Joker and 3 other cards; scissors; glue.*

1. Cut the Joker in half diagonally.

2. Glue one half to the face of one other card.

3. Put the three cards together, face up. The prepared card should be at the bottom of the three cards.

❚ Hold the cards together, face up. Pull the bottom card to the left, keeping the top two cards together so they look like just one card. It should look as if you are holding three cards, the middle one of which is the Joker.

2 Turn the cards over, face down. As you do this, use your fingers to spread the three cards apart.

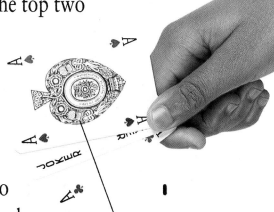

Two top cards held together

3 Ask someone to take the Joker from the face-down cards. He or she will take the center card.

4 Push the two remaining cards together so that when you turn them face up again, the half Joker is hidden. It looks as if you are holding two ordinary cards.

5 Ask the spectator to turn over the card that he or she has taken. It is not the Joker! The Joker has disappeared!

✔ *This trick needs careful practice so you can hide the Joker perfectly. Talk and joke with the audience so that they don't look too closely at the cards!*

JUMP!

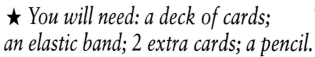

A chosen card leaps from the deck!

★ *You will need: a deck of cards; an elastic band; 2 extra cards; a pencil.*

1. With the pencil, make a small hole in the center of each extra card.

2. Cut the elastic band and push one end through each of the holes in the cards.

3. Tie knots in each end of the band.

4. Push the prepared cards into the deck.

1 Spread the cards out, face down. Ask someone to take any card. Hide the prepared cards within the deck, so that he or she does not try to take either of them.

2 Ask the spectator to show the card to the audience. While this is being done, secretly find the special cards and push the tip of your finger between them.

1

2

3 Ask the spectator to return the card. To help him or her, make a gap between the special cards so the card is placed between them. Push the card in until it fits into the rest of the pack.

This stretches the elastic band. Hold the pack tightly to stop the chosen card from jumping out.

3

4 Tell the audience that you have amazing magical powers. Ask them for the name of the chosen card. Shout "Jump!" and at the same time loosen your grip. The chosen card will leap out!

Card forces elastic band down

✔ *Try this several times before showing it to anyone. You may have to alter the length of the elastic band a few times until you find the best one to use.*

Word POWER

Spell the names of cards... and watch them appear!

★ *You will need: 10 playing cards – ace to nine and a Joker.*
*1. Pile the cards facing up in this order: 4 (on the bottom), 9,
Joker, A, 3, 6, 8, 2, 5, 7 on the top.*
*2. Put the pile, face down on the deck, so that the audience are
not suspicious. Pick up the top 10 cards to start the trick.*

1 Say the letters "A, C, E." As you say each
one, take a card from the top of the pile and put it
on the bottom. After "E," show the next card – it's an ace.
Put this card down on the table, face up.

2 Repeat this, but say the letters "T, W, O." The next
card turned up will be a two. Again, put this on the table.

3 Keep repeating this, with the numbers three to nine,
until one card is left in your hand.
Say "This card should be a ten
– but to spell ten with one card
would be a joke." Turn over
the card... to show the Joker!

Top DOG

The card that's determined to be the best!

1 Take two cards from the deck, but hold them together so that they look like a single card. Show them to the audience so that only the lower card is seen – the Ace of Hearts, for example.

2 cards

2 Say "The Ace of Hearts (or whichever card is seen) thinks it's the most important card in the deck."

3 Put the two cards together on top of the deck.

4 Say "Even if you try to make it an ordinary card, it always wants to be top dog." As you say this, take the top card (just one) and push it into the center of the deck. The audience will think it is the Ace, so don't let them see it!

5 As you say "top dog," turn over the top card – it's the Ace of Hearts!

✔ *Practice holding the two cards as one. Time what you say so that it fits exactly with what you are doing.*

Sticky FINGERS

Your hands have magnetic powers!

★ *You will need: a deck of cards; 2 extra cards; scissors; glue.*

1. *Cut a small square from the center of one extra card.*

2. *Fold this square in half and glue one half of it to the back of the other card, to make a special card with a small flap on its back.*

3. *Flatten out the flap so that the card is not much thicker than an ordinary one, and put it on top of the deck.*

❙ Place the special card face up in the palm of your hand. As you do so, secretly open the small flap and squeeze it between your fingers.

2 Put several other cards in your hand, secretly slipping them under the special card.

3 Turn your hand over so that your palm faces the floor. The cards will not fall to the floor, as the audience expects, because they will be held firmly in place by the special card. Keep gripping the flap as tightly as possible.

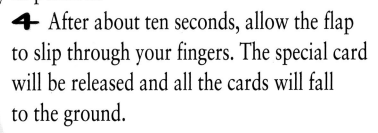

4 After about ten seconds, allow the flap to slip through your fingers. The special card will be released and all the cards will fall to the ground.

✔ *When you turn your hand over, some of the cards may fall. Don't worry – this makes the trick look more impossible! When you gather the cards after the trick, look for the special card and secretly flatten the flap. Pick up the cards with the special one hidden among them.*

Through the MIDDLE

A card is pushed through the center of another.

★ *You will need: 3 cards (two of which should be cards of the same value and suit); scissors; glue.*
1. *Cut one of the similar cards in half diagonally.*
2. *Put glue on the top and bottom corners of its back.*
3. *Stick the half card onto the face of the other similar card, so that the edges of the two cards are together.*

❶ Show the special card and one other card to the audience.

2 Pretend to put the ordinary card behind the special card. In fact, you should push it slowly into the unglued part of the special card, so that it passes between the half card and the card that is glued to its back.

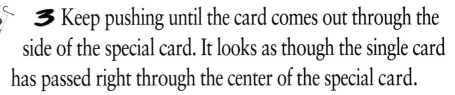

3 Keep pushing until the card comes out through the side of the special card. It looks as though the single card has passed right through the center of the special card.

✔ *Have the special card ready on the top of the deck. The audience will think it is an ordinary card.*

Seeing with your FINGERS

Just by rubbing a card, you can tell the audience what it is.

1 Give the deck to a volunteer and ask him or her to give you just one card.

2 Hold the card in your right hand, with your fingers at one end and your thumb at the other. It should have its back facing you.

3 Raise your left fingers to touch the face of the card. Pretend to feel the ink with your fingertips.

4 Secretly bend the card so you can see the corner number. Pretend to concentrate hard, then name the card.

✔ *This works best if you do it more than once, with different cards.*

The Balancing CARD

Stand a card up – and balance a glass on it!

★ *You will need: 2 cards; glue; a plastic wine glass.*
1. *Bend one card in half lengthwise.*
2. *Glue one half onto the back of the other card to make a movable flap. Flatten it and put it in the pack.*

1 Take the special card from the deck.

2 Pretend that you are trying to balance the card on the table. Let it fall over a few times to make the trick more convincing. Secretly open the flap.

3 Stand the card on the table, then pick up the wine glass and balance it on top of the card.

✔ *Never do this trick if there are people on either side of you. To make it even more impressive, pour water into the glass as it balances on the card.*

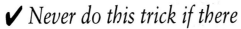

The Card VANISHES

A card is chosen – and disappears!

★ *You will need: a deck of cards; a lip protection stick.*
Wipe the lip protector in an "X" on the back of the top card.

1 Ask a volunteer to take a card. ~~Make sure that~~ he or she does not ~~take~~ the ~~top card~~.

2 Ask him or her to show the card to the rest of the audience then put it back on the top of the deck.

3 Secretly give the deck a squeeze. Shuffle the cards, keeping the chosen card and prepared card together.

4 Ask the audience for the name of the chosen card. Say "That's strange, this pack doesn't have (the chosen card)."

5 Turn the deck face up and count out the cards onto the table. The chosen card will stick to the prepared card. Handle them together as if they are one card.

6 Keep counting out the cards until they are all on the table – the chosen card has vanished!

Manuscript MAGIC

An ancient text reveals a chosen card!

★ *You will need: a deck of cards; paper; tea bags; a pen.*

1. *Ask an adult to make some tea in a bowl. Let it cool, then soak the paper overnight. Allow it to dry. This will make the paper look old.*

2. *Fold the paper in half, then fold the top layer of paper back on itself.*

2. *Write the name of a card over the point where the paper is folded. It doesn't matter which card you write. For now, let's use the seven of spades.*

3. *Open the paper and you will have two columns of strange marks. Make these marks into ancient-looking writing. Put another column of similar writing in between them.*

❚ Ask a volunteer to choose a card from your deck. In fact, you should "force" (see pages 8-9) the seven of spades.

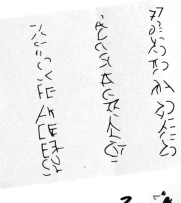

2

2 Show the paper to the audience and say that it names the chosen card. Ask for the name of the card. When the spectator says "seven of spades," reply "Yes, that is what this ancient manuscript says – seven of spades."

3 Fold the paper so that the two halves of your original writing come together. Everyone can see that the manuscript really did foretell which card would be chosen!

✔ *It is a good idea to make several of these papers, using a different card name each time. It will look very suspicious if you use the same card every time you do the trick!*

Boxing CLEVER

Wave your hand... and a card changes into a box!

★ *You will need: a card; a small box; glue; paint.*

1. Glue the card to the top of the box and fold it in half. Ask an adult to score along the folds with a knife.

2. Paint or decorate the back of the card so that it looks like the top of the box.

3. Open the card and flatten it.

❶ Show the open card to the audience, keeping the box hidden behind it.

❷ Wave your hand over the card and fold it up as you do so – the card has changed into a box.

✔ *You could put a coin into the box, and hold it in place with clay. Take it out after the trick and tell the audience that it is your payment!*

1

2

One Way to DO IT

Use your magical powers to find a card!

★ *You will need: a deck of cards with pictures on the backs (the same picture on all the cards).*
Sort the cards so that all the pictures are the same way up.

1 Spread out the cards and ask someone to take any card.

2 Ask him or her to show it to the rest of the audience.

3 Ask him or her to push the card back into the deck. Make sure that the picture on the back is facing in the opposite way to the rest. Most people will turn the card around before they push it back. If not, quickly turn the cards in your hands before the card is returned.

4 Hold the cards in a fan, the faces toward the audience. Look at the backs and find the upside-down card. That is the chosen card.

✔ *Practice turning the cards quickly and secretly.*

3

The chosen card

4

The Disappearing QUEEN

A card vanishes into thin air!

★ *You will need: 4 playing cards (2 of the cards must be the same and one card must be a Queen); scissors; glue; a handkerchief.*

1. Take the two cards that are the same and glue them together, back to back.

2. Cut the Queen in half lengthwise.

3. Glue half of the Queen to the edge of the double card you have made.

4. Place the third card over the face of the Queen and slightly to one side. It should look as if you are holding three cards and the middle one is the Queen.

❙ Hold the cards carefully so that they look like three cards. Show the audience that the Queen is in the middle.

❷ Cover the cards with the handkerchief.

3 Reach under the handkerchief. Before you pull the cards out, quickly and secretly turn over the special card so that the ordinary side is facing forward.

4 Reach under the handkerchief again and take out the ordinary card. Everyone will think that the Queen is still under the handkerchief.

5 Make some magic passes over the handkerchief, then lift it up dramatically. The Queen has disappeared!

✔ *Keep your hand rigid to make the audience think the Queen is still there. If you have another Queen of the same suit, hide it in a book, for example. When the Queen disappears, make some magic gestures toward the hiding place and then go and pick up the card.*

CARD TRICK WORDS

Ace A card with the value of one.

Audience The people who come to watch your show.

Cut Dividing the deck.

Deck A set of playing cards: 4 suits of 13 cards, plus extra Jokers.

Face card A "royal" card (Queen, King or Jack).

"Forcing" Making someone pick the card you want from the deck.

Joker An extra card in a deck, with a jester on it.

Shuffling Mixing the cards so they are in a random order in the deck.

Suit A "family" of cards – spades, clubs, hearts, or diamonds.

INDEX

More Card Trick IDEAS

If you want to invent some of your own card tricks, try changing or combining the tricks you know already. There are hundreds of books in stores and libraries to give you more ideas.